JOHN F. KENNEDY

The new president had everything. He came from a rich family, with a strong father who wanted his children to do well. He was charming and intelligent, with a beautiful young wife and two lovely children. He was a war hero, with an award for courage. And when he gave speeches, people listened and believed in what he said. Surely, Americans thought, John F. Kennedy was a great leader for a great country.

But not everything was so easy. JFK wanted world peace, but there was trouble in Germany, Cuba, and Vietnam. Many Americans fought against the idea of equal rights for black Americans. And a president must be president, even when his back hurts and he is secretly ill.

And all the time, the sudden end of Kennedy's extraordinary time as president was coming closer and closer . . .

OXFORD BOOKWORMS LIBRARY

Factfiles

John F. Kennedy

Stage 2 (700 headwords)

Factfiles Series Editor: Christine Lindop

ANNE COLLINS

John F. Kennedy

OXFORD UNIVERSITY PRESS

OXFORD
UNIVERSITY PRESS

Great Clarendon Street, Oxford, OX2 6DP, United Kingdom

Oxford University Press is a department of the University of Oxford.
It furthers the University's objective of excellence in research, scholarship,
and education by publishing worldwide. Oxford is a registered trade
mark of Oxford University Press in the UK and in certain other countries

ISBN: 978 0 19 423672 0

A complete recording of *John F. Kennedy* is available.

Printed in China

Word count (main text): 6,857

For more information on the Oxford Bookworms Library,
visit www.oup.com/elt/gradedreaders

ACKNOWLEDGEMENTS

Cover image courtesy of: Corbis (John F. Kennedy/John Bryson/Sygma)
Maps by: Peter Bull pp.2, 18, 23
The publishers would like to thank the following for their permission to reproduce photographs:
Alamy pp.6 (Keystone Pictures USA), 7 (Stocktrek Images, Inc), 12 (Keystone Pictures USA),
16 (Everett Collection Historical), 17 (Keystone Pictures USA), 20 (Interfoto), 28 (Charles O Cecil),
29 (Everett Collection Historical), 31 (Everett Collection Historical), 32 (Stocktrek Images, Inc),
36 (RGB Ventures LLC dba Superstock), 37 (Universal Images Group Limited); Corbis UK Ltd pp.1,
5 (Bettmann), 8, 13, 14 (Bettmann), 21, 26, 34, 38 (Bettmann), 41 (Bettmann); Mary Evans Picture
Library pp.4 (Friedrich/Interfoto), 19 (Everett Collection); Getty Images pp.10 (National Archive/
Newsmakers), 24 (Keystone), 25 (Central Press), 33 (Three Lions), 35 (SSPL/NASA), 40 (Kevin Clark/
The Washington Post)

CONTENTS

1 A great president

John F. Kennedy was the thirty-fifth president of the United States. He was president for only a short time, from 20 January 1961 to 22 November 1963. But he is one of the best loved American presidents ever, together with Abraham Lincoln and Theodore Roosevelt. When he died suddenly, he was still a young man, only forty-six years old. His death was a terrible shock for people in the US and around the world.

Kennedy's full name was John Fitzgerald Kennedy, but people often call him JFK. He was the second youngest man to become president of the US (Theodore Roosevelt, at forty-two, was younger by a year). There are many interesting 'firsts' about Kennedy. He was the first American president to be born in the 1900s. He was the first Catholic president, and the first president to win a Pulitzer Prize, a special award from Columbia University, for a book that he wrote (the book was called *Profiles in Courage*, and it was about eight US senators who showed political courage). He was also the first US president to die before his mother and father.

John F. Kennedy died more than fifty years ago, but the world still remembers him. There are many books about him, and in 1991 Oliver Stone made a film, *JFK*, about his death. Important buildings and other places carry his name. Perhaps the most famous is the John F. Kennedy

International Airport in New York, but there is also the John F. Kennedy Space Center, John F. Kennedy University, and many schools. The government of Canada even called a mountain by his name: Mount Kennedy in the Kluane National Park in the Yukon.

But why did people love Kennedy so much? He was a strong leader who wanted to do his best for his country. He was intelligent and he worked hard. He was good-looking and charming. People liked him and they believed in his ideas. He was also very good at giving speeches. If you listen to Kennedy's famous speeches today, you can easily understand why people admired him. He gave them hope for the future.

This is the story of John F. Kennedy.

2 The Kennedys

In 1849, a young Irishman, Patrick Kennedy, left Ireland and traveled to the US by ship. At that time, there were terrible problems in Ireland. The most important food for poor people was potatoes. But in the late 1840s, the potatoes went bad, and many people had nothing to eat. About a million Irish people died, and another million left Ireland. Many of these went to the US, hoping for a better life.

Patrick Kennedy found work in Boston, Massachusetts, in the east of the US. He married and had five children. His children married, and they had children too. The Kennedys were very hard-working, and over the years, they made a lot of money in business. They also became an important political family.

One of Patrick Kennedy's grandsons was called Joseph, or Joe. In October 1914, Joe married Rose Fitzgerald. The Fitzgeralds, like the Kennedys, were one of Boston's most important political families. Joe and Rose had nine children – four boys and five girls. Their first son, Joe, was born on 25 July 1915, and their second son on 29 May 1917. His full name was John Fitzgerald Kennedy, but sometimes his friends and family called him Jack.

The Kennedys were rich, so their life was comfortable. For most of the year, they lived in a big house in Boston. They had another family home in Hyannis Port on Cape

The young Kennedys (JFK second from right)

Cod, where they went every summer. The children spent happy times swimming, sailing, and playing sports.

Joe Kennedy Senior had big plans for his large family. He wanted his children to win at everything, and he pushed them to do their best. He had great hopes for them all, but his greatest hopes were for his oldest son.

'One day my son Joe is going to be president,' he said.

Joe was a very important person in Jack's life too. He admired his older brother very much. When Jack was thirteen, he entered the Choate School in Connecticut, a very good school for boys. Joe was already at the school, and everybody liked him. He was intelligent, good-looking and a football star. People liked Jack too, but he was not always a good student. He was intelligent, and he loved sports, but he did not always work hard. Sometimes he and his friends got into trouble. Jack was often ill too. He hurt his back playing football, and he had problems because of other illnesses. Sometimes he could not go to school for weeks.

After leaving Choate, Jack followed Joe to Harvard University. Then something very exciting happened for the Kennedy family. The US president at that time, President Franklin D. Roosevelt, sent Joe Kennedy Senior to the UK as ambassador for the US. So in 1938, the Kennedys moved to London. Joe and Jack were still students at Harvard, but they came to stay with their family in the summer holidays.

JFK, Joe Kennedy Senior, and Joe Kennedy

The US ambassador had a very important job. In the late 1930s, many things were changing in Europe. Adolf Hitler was leader of Germany, and he was friendly with Benito Mussolini, leader of Italy. Hitler and Mussolini had dangerous ideas. They planned to control other countries in Europe, and many people were worried that there would be war. As US ambassador to London, Joe Kennedy Senior had to find out what was happening in the UK and Europe, and tell the US government. He had meetings with important people, and his sons met these people too. Jack became very interested in different countries and their governments.

American official Sumner Welles, British Prime Minister Winston Churchill, and Joe Kennedy Senior

3   A war hero

On 1 September 1939 the German army attacked Poland, and World War Two began.

In September 1941, Jack joined the US Navy. Three months later, on 8 December 1941, the US entered World War Two. Jack's older brother, Joe, was already in the navy, flying war planes in Europe. After Jack finished training as a navy officer, the navy sent him to the South Pacific as leader of a patrol torpedo boat, the *PT-109*.

In World War Two, the Americans and the Japanese were enemies. There was often heavy fighting between American and Japanese ships near the Solomon Islands, a group of islands east of Papua New Guinea. The Japanese had a lot of soldiers on these islands. The food and other things that they needed came to the islands on Japanese warships.

In the navy

JFK on the *PT-109*

The American patrol boats had to try and stop these warships. When they found one, they attacked it with torpedoes. This was a very dangerous job because the patrol boats were much smaller than the Japanese ships.

At about 2.30 a.m. on 2 August 1943, Jack's boat, the *PT-109*, was near the islands. The night was very dark with no moon or stars, and it was difficult to see anything. Suddenly, the men had a terrible shock. A large Japanese warship, the *Amagiri*, came out of the black night, very near the *PT-109*. Jack was holding the wheel of the boat. He turned it as quickly as he could, trying to move the *PT-109* out of the *Amagiri*'s way.

But it was too late. The *Amagiri* crashed into the *PT-109*, and cut it into two pieces. A big fire started and two of Jack's men died. Jack and the other men jumped into the sea. Some of the men had terrible burns on their faces and bodies. Jack had no burns, but his back was badly hurt in the crash. Jack and his men were in the water, holding on to pieces of the *PT-109*.

'What do you want to do, men?' Jack asked. 'A lot of you have families, and some of you have children. I have nothing to lose. So you must decide. Do you want to fight, or surrender to the Japanese?'

'We will never surrender!' said the men.

The men thought that the US Navy would send a plane to look for them. They waited and waited, but no plane came. So the next morning, Jack told his men to swim to an island about five kilometres away. The swim was long and very difficult, and it took them five hours to get to the island. Two of the men could not swim, so the others pulled them. One man, Patrick McMahon, had terrible burns. Jack was a strong swimmer and he pulled McMahon behind him. Jack was very tired and his back was hurting, so every few minutes he stopped for a rest. Each time he stopped, McMahon asked:

'How far is it now, Mr Kennedy?'

'We're doing fine,' Kennedy always replied. 'How do you feel, Mac?'

McMahon always answered, 'I'm OK, Mr Kennedy. How about you?'

Jack pulled McMahon to the island and the other men followed. But when they arrived, they found that the island was very small. So after resting they decided to swim to a larger island, where there was food and water. A few days later, some islanders found them and went to get help.

After Jack arrived back in the US, he became a war hero. The US government gave him an award for courage, and for being a strong leader. Everybody admired Jack for saving the lives of McMahon and the other men. But he never thought of himself as a big hero. When people asked Jack, 'How did you become a war hero?' he just laughed. 'It was easy,' he said. 'They cut my PT boat in half.'

Jack's older brother, Joe, also got awards for courage. But later in the war, a terrible thing happened. On 12 August 1944, Joe was killed while he was flying on a dangerous job in Europe.

JFK (right) and the men from the *PT-109*

4   To the White House

Joe's death was a great shock for Joe Kennedy Senior. He was hoping that his oldest son would be president of the US one day. But after Joe died, his hopes turned to Jack.

After World War Two ended in 1945, Jack got a job with a newspaper. He went to San Francisco and wrote about an important United Nations meeting. Then he went to the UK and wrote about the elections there. But Jack did not want to be a newsman; he wanted to get into Congress.

The government of the US has three different parts: the President, Congress, and the Supreme Court. The President is the most important person in the US government; he is the head of the country, and the head of the army. There are two 'houses' in Congress – the House of Representatives and the Senate – and they make the laws. The Supreme Court decides what the laws mean.

There are only two important political parties: the Republicans and the Democrats. At that time, after the war, the Republicans wanted people to work to help themselves, but the Democrats wanted the government to help when it was needed. The Kennedys were a strong Democratic family. In 1946, there was an election in Massachusetts to choose someone for the House of Representatives, and the Democrats chose Jack as their candidate. He won the election easily.

Jack stayed in the House of Representatives for six years, then he won an election to the Senate. In 1953, the year when Jack became a senator, Dwight D. Eisenhower, the Republican candidate, became US president. But nobody can be president for more than eight years, so in November 1960, there was an election for a new president. The Democrats chose Jack as their presidential candidate.

By this time, Jack understood many things about government because of his work as a senator. He was also becoming famous, and his picture was often in the newspapers. The American people were very interested in the good-looking young Senator Kennedy, and they enjoyed reading stories about him and his family. They also admired him because he was a war hero.

JFK speaks while Jackie watches

The months before the presidential elections were very exciting for the Kennedys. Jack needed a lot of votes to win against the Republican party. He worked very hard, traveling all over the US, giving speeches and telling people about himself. Jack's father, Joe Kennedy Senior, and his younger brother Robert often went with him. Joe spent a lot of money helping Jack.

The candidate for the Republican party was Richard Nixon. Nixon was older than Jack, and this was his eighth year as vice president – the person who takes control if the president is ill. In September and October, Jack and Nixon went on TV together to talk about why each man wanted to be president. Jack looked very good, but Nixon looked tired and uncomfortable. After people saw the two candidates on TV, more people wanted Jack to be president than Nixon.

Nixon and JFK on TV

In the presidential elections on 8 November 1960, 34,226,925 people voted for Jack and 34,108,662 voted for Nixon. So Jack won the election and became President John F. Kennedy, thirty-fifth president of the United States. He was forty-three years old. On 20 January 1961, the new president gave a very famous and important speech. Many Americans remembered this speech for a long time. Kennedy talked about the need for Americans to help their country.

'Ask not what your country can do for you, ask what you can do for your country,' he said.

The people listened and they felt full of hope. Their new president was going to be a great leader. It was a new start for the US.

'Ask what you can do for your country.'

5 The First Lady

Kennedy met his wife, Jacqueline Bouvier, at a dinner party in New York in 1952. They fell in love, and married on 12 September 1953, when Kennedy was a senator.

Jacqueline, or Jackie, was beautiful and intelligent. Her family came to America from France in the early 1800s. Like the Kennedys, they worked hard and made a lot of money in business. Jackie was born on 28 July 1929. When she was a little girl, she loved horses and riding. She also enjoyed reading, dancing, and learning French. While she was a student, she went to Paris for a year and lived with a French family. When Jackie met Kennedy, she had a job with the *Washington Times-Herald* newspaper. She took photos of interesting and famous people, and wrote stories about them.

When Kennedy became the presidential candidate for the Democrats, Jackie helped him. He traveled to many places in the US and Jackie often went too. She was very good at talking to people, and she was charming. People liked Jackie a lot. She talked to newspapers, and wrote hundreds of letters, telling people about her husband.

JFK and Jackie marry

The wife of the US president is called the First Lady. In early 1961, the new president and his First Lady moved into the White House, home of the US president in Washington since 1800. The White House was a beautiful building, but many of the rooms were not very interesting. So Jackie decided to give the White House a new look, and she brought pictures and other things from all over America. When everything was ready, 80 million Americans watched Jackie on TV, showing the White House to the country.

Kennedy and Jackie were different from other US presidents and First Ladies. In some ways, they were like film stars. They were young and good-looking, and their pictures were often in the newspapers. The American people were very interested in the Kennedys, and they enjoyed reading about them. Many women admired Jackie's clothes. When Kennedy visited other countries,

Jackie often went too and met heads of government. The Kennedys also had dinner parties at the White House. Many people came – not only important political people, but also people famous in music and film.

But not everything in the Kennedys' lives was happy. In 1956, Jackie had a daughter, but the little girl was born dead. Then they had two more children – Caroline, born in 1957, and John, born in 1960. In 1963, Jackie had another baby, Patrick, but he only lived for two days. And Kennedy still had bad problems with his back and other illnesses.

Jackie wanted to help her husband and do her best for her country, but she also wanted to be a good mother. She wanted the White House to be a real home for her children. She made one of the rooms into a small school for Caroline and ten other children. In the garden there was a tree house where Caroline and John could play. The White House was the president's house, but it was a family home too.

JFK with Caroline and John in the White House

6   The Cold War

One of Kennedy's most difficult problems was America's relationship with the USSR. After World War Two ended, the US and the USSR became two of the most important countries in the world. Both countries were very strong politically, and both had large armies and nuclear weapons. But they had very different ways of government.

The USSR – also called the Soviet Union – was a Communist country. In Communist countries, there is only one political party – the Communist party. People can only vote for candidates from this party. The US was against Communism. It did not agree with the Communist way of life, and it thought that Communist ideas were dangerous.

After World War Two, the relationship between the US and the USSR got worse. In a way, the two countries were at war with each other, but there was no open fighting between Soviet soldiers (from the USSR) and US soldiers. So this war was called 'the Cold War'. On one side was the US, and countries in the west of Europe like Britain and France. On the other side was the USSR, and the countries that it controlled in the east of Europe.

In June 1961, Kennedy asked the leader of the USSR, Nikita Khrushchev, to meet him in Vienna for talks. He was hoping that the US could begin a better relationship with the USSR. Most of all, he wanted to talk to Khrushchev about an important problem – Berlin.

After World War Two, the US, Britain, France, and the USSR divided Germany into four parts. The USSR controlled one part, and the US, Britain, and France controlled the other three parts. Berlin was in the part of Germany which the USSR controlled. Berlin was also in two parts. The USSR controlled East Berlin, and the other three countries controlled West Berlin.

Khrushchev and JFK
in Vienna, 1961

The USSR was a Communist country, so the government of East Berlin was Communist too. But many citizens of East Berlin did not want to live under a Communist government. So they started leaving East Berlin and going to West Berlin to look for jobs. Between 1947 and 1961,

about 3 million people left East Berlin. Khrushchev was very angry about this.

Kennedy hoped that he and Khrushchev could talk about Berlin in a friendly way, but the talks did not go well. Kennedy and Khrushchev were very different men. Khrushchev, leader of the Soviets since 1953, was sixty-seven, more than twenty years older than Kennedy. He was not from a rich political family like the Kennedys; he was a working man from a small village in the Soviet Union. He thought that Kennedy was intelligent, but too young and soft.

After the talks, Kennedy felt worried and unhappy. He and Khrushchev could not agree about Berlin. Kennedy did not know what Khrushchev was planning to do. The Soviets wanted to stop people leaving East Berlin and going to West Berlin. Were they planning to attack West Berlin?

'If the Soviets attack West Berlin,' Kennedy thought worriedly, 'then the US will have to protect it. We'll have to fight the Soviets.'

But Khrushchev did not want open war. He had another plan. On 12 August 1961, two months after the Vienna

Building the Berlin Wall

talks, East German soldiers worked hard all night. In the morning, the citizens of Berlin had a big shock. There was a wall around West Berlin! The wall divided many people from their friends and families in the other part of Berlin.

The Berlin Wall shocked people all over the world. During the next few years, about 5,000 people escaped from East Berlin to West Berlin. But it was not easy to get over the wall. There were soldiers with guns along the wall, and they shot anyone who tried to escape. Many people in Berlin were angry with the US. Why didn't the US protect the citizens of East Berlin? But Kennedy said the US could only help the citizens of West Berlin.

In June 1963, Kennedy went to West Berlin and stood in front of the wall. There were a million people on the street, trying to see the president. Later, in a famous speech, he said, '*Ich bin ein Berliner*' ('I am a citizen of Berlin'). He told people why the East German way of government could never work. He said that it was not always easy to be free, but 'we never had to put a wall up to keep our people in.'

Kennedy promised that the US would go on helping the citizens of West Berlin. They were very happy with him, and Kennedy was happy too. When he left Berlin, he said to a friend, 'We'll never have another day like this one, as long as we live.'

JFK speaks to West Berlin

7   Problems in Cuba

In April 1961, three months after Kennedy became president, he had a big problem with Cuba.

The government of Cuba was Communist. The US president before Kennedy, President Eisenhower, was very worried about Fidel Castro, the leader of Cuba. He thought that Castro was very dangerous. Cuba is in the Caribbean Sea, near to the state of Florida, in the south of the US. Castro had a strong army, and Eisenhower was worried that he was planning to attack the US.

But Eisenhower did not want to start a war with Cuba openly. So he made a plan with his military advisors and the Central Intelligence Agency (CIA). There were nearly 1,500 Cubans living in the US who did not agree with Castro's government, and who were ready to fight him.

'If the US army trains these Cubans,' thought Eisenhower, 'we can send them to attack Castro. But we will not use US soldiers in the attack.'

When Kennedy became president in 1961, the military advisors told him to go on with Eisenhower's plan.

'Most people in Cuba are against Castro,' the advisors told Kennedy. 'When the Cuban soldiers arrive from the US, the Cuban people will join the soldiers and fight with them against Castro.'

Kennedy was not sure that the military advisors were right, but he agreed to their plan. On 17 April 1961, five

ships carrying about 1,500 Cuban soldiers arrived at a place called the Bay of Pigs. But everything went wrong. Castro found out that they were coming, and he had an army of 20,000 soldiers waiting. Nearly three hundred soldiers from the two armies were killed, and over a thousand Cuban soldiers from the US surrendered to Castro's army.

When he heard what happened, Kennedy was very unhappy. He felt sorry about the Cubans who died, and the others who were now in an army prison in Cuba. He learned an important lesson from the Bay of Pigs. In the future, he did not agree to do everything that his military advisors and the CIA told him.

Castro and Khrushchev

In 1962, Kennedy had an even bigger problem. Cuba and the USSR were both Communist countries, and Castro was very friendly with the Soviet leader, Khrushchev. The US had some nuclear missile sites in Turkey. Khrushchev was worried that the US would attack the USSR from these missile sites, so he talked to Castro.

'Will you allow us to build some nuclear missile sites on Cuba?' he asked.

Castro agreed to help Khrushchev, so the Soviets started moving thousands of soldiers and weapons to Cuba. The US wanted to find out what was happening. Why were so many Soviet ships arriving in Cuba? On 14 October Kennedy sent a plane with a camera over Cuba. It came back with pictures that showed the missile sites.

When Kennedy saw the pictures, he immediately called meetings of his military advisors, the CIA, and other important people in the US government. The meetings went on for a long time. Everyone had different ideas about what to do.

'We must send planes to Cuba immediately,' said the military advisors. 'We must attack these missile sites.' But Kennedy remembered the Bay of Pigs. He did not want to decide anything too quickly.

'No,' he said. 'If we attack the missile sites, the USSR will attack the US. There will be nuclear war and millions of people will die. We must find another way.'

At last they agreed on a plan. Many Soviet ships were arriving in Cuba, carrying men and weapons. Kennedy sent a letter to Khrushchev.

'The US Navy is going to stop your ships,' he said. 'If we find any weapons on them, we will stop them from entering Cuba.'

At the same time, Kennedy told the US Army and Navy to be ready for war. He sent 125,000 soldiers to Florida.

Nuclear missiles in Moscow

JFK and his advisors

He told the US Air Force to get ready to attack Cuba and the USSR. People all over the world were very worried. Angry crowds held meetings against the US in London and some countries in Europe.

'What will the US do if the Soviet ships don't stop?' they asked. 'Will there be nuclear war?'

But Khrushchev, like Kennedy, did not want nuclear war. He told the Soviet ships to stop and turn back when they met the US ships. Then he sent Kennedy two letters. The first letter said: 'We promise to take away our nuclear missiles from Cuba, but you must promise that the US will never attack Cuba.'

The second letter said: 'The US must promise to take away its nuclear missiles in Turkey.'

Kennedy wrote back to Khrushchev, agreeing openly to the first letter. He also agreed to the second letter, but secretly.

Many people admired Kennedy for stopping a nuclear war with the USSR. In November 1962, there were elections, and Kennedy's party, the Democrats, got more votes than before. And Khrushchev learned something about the new US president. He learned that Kennedy was a strong leader.

8 Peace and war

Kennedy's greatest hope was for world peace. He fought in World War Two himself, and he saw that war was a terrible thing in which millions of people died. His older brother, Joe, was killed in war. Kennedy did not want to start another war, and he did not want to go to war only because his military advisors told him to.

'If countries can understand each other better,' he thought, 'they will not be so ready to fight.'

Kennedy began to think of ways that he could help world peace. Soon after he became president in 1961, he had a wonderful new idea. He started the Peace Corps for young Americans who wanted to do something to help another country.

The Peace Corps is still going on today. Young people who join the Peace Corps travel to countries like Jamaica, Ghana, and Indonesia. They live there for two years, working with the people in that country and helping them. They do not get any money, but they learn about that country, and the people there learn about the US. Since 1961, more than 200,000 young Americans have joined the Peace Corps. Both Republican and Democratic governments agree that the Peace Corps is a very good thing, and give money to it.

Kennedy did other things to help peace too. On 10 June 1963, he made a famous speech, the Peace

Young Americans in the Peace Corps

Speech, at American University in Washington, D.C. He talked about the dangers of nuclear war, and the need for countries to live side by side in peace.

But there was still trouble in some parts of the world. One big problem was Vietnam in Southeast Asia. North Vietnam was a Communist country, but South Vietnam was not. North Vietnam had a strong army, the NLF, which wanted to control South Vietnam, and was already controlling many villages.

President Eisenhower and his government were very worried about North Vietnam. They were afraid that the North Vietnamese Communists would control first South Vietnam, and then other countries in Asia. So they sent money and military advisors to help the South Vietnamese government. When Kennedy became president, his government went on helping South Vietnam.

The leader of the South Vietnamese government was a Catholic politician called Ngô Đình Diệm. But sometimes there were problems with Diệm. In 1961, Kennedy sent money to Diệm, who used it to train more soldiers and make the South Vietnamese army stronger.

The US also sent military advisors and soldiers to help with the training. Diệm trained more soldiers, but he did not use his new army against the Communists; he used it against other Vietnamese who were not Catholics. Many people in Vietnam were very angry and unhappy with Diệm.

After that, the US government did not want to help Diệm any more. They learned that some officers in Diệm's army were planning to put a new leader in Diệm's place. The US said it would not stop the army officers, but they wanted to protect Diệm. The army officers promised that Diệm would not be hurt, but then they shot Diệm and his brother. Diệm's death was a great shock for Kennedy.

In September 1963, the world moved closer to peace. Both the US and USSR had nuclear weapons. After Kennedy became president, he tried many times to get the Soviets to stop testing their weapons. But the Soviets did not stop, so the US went on testing their nuclear weapons too. Then, by October 1963, both sides agreed to stop the tests. Many people saw this as the start of a better relationship between the two countries, and they were very happy with Kennedy.

Eisenhower (left) and Diệm (right) in 1957

9   Equal rights for all

Kennedy also had problems at home. The biggest problem in the US was equal rights.

Some states in the US – many of them in the south – did not believe in equal rights for black Americans. They did not allow black Americans to eat in the same restaurants as white Americans, or travel on the same buses, or buy things in the same shops. The police sometimes helped the black Americans, but often they did nothing. In 1954, the Supreme Court said that it was against the law to stop black children from going to the same schools as white children. But in the states in the south many schools did not agree with this, and they did not let black children in.

Kennedy strongly believed in equal rights for black and white people. Before he became president, he promised the black Americans that he would help them. So in the presidential elections, most black Americans voted for Kennedy. But after he became president, he became busy with other problems, like Cuba and the Cold War. Many black Americans became angry with him.

'Kennedy wanted us to vote for him,' they said. 'But now he isn't interested in our problems.'

But it was difficult for Kennedy to help the black Americans. He wanted a strong new law about equal rights. But he knew that the Democrats from the states in the south would stop the law going through Congress.

In 1961 and 1962, the problems between black Americans and white Americans got worse. There was fighting; many people were hurt and some were killed.

In September 1962, a young black man, James Meredith, became a student at the University of Mississippi. All the other students were white. When Meredith first went to the university, nobody allowed him to enter. Kennedy's younger brother, Robert, was Attorney General, head of law in the US. He sent 400 men to the university to protect Meredith. There was a big fight; two people were killed, and many others were hurt. Then the president sent 3,000 soldiers to protect Meredith. This was very important for the black Americans. It showed them that Kennedy was ready to help them.

James Meredith arrives at the University of Mississippi

In 1963, two young black students, Vivian Malone and James Hood, became students at the University of Alabama. On 11 June, they went to pay their money to the university. But the Governor of Alabama, George Wallace, stood in the doorway with his soldiers, and did not allow them to enter. Again, Kennedy sent soldiers from Washington, and Wallace had to allow the students in.

That evening, Kennedy gave a famous speech on TV and radio about equal rights. He said that all Americans must be able to eat lunch in the same restaurants, send

JFK speaks about equal rights, 11 June 1961

their children to the best schools, and vote. He said the US 'will not be fully free until all its citizens are free.' He also said he was planning an important new law about equal rights for different groups of Americans.

On 28 August 1963, about 250,000 people, mostly black Americans, came together in Washington for a big meeting. Kennedy was worried that there would be trouble, so he had soldiers ready. But there was no trouble, and the crowds walked through the streets of Washington in peace. One of the leaders was the churchman Martin Luther King Junior, who gave a famous speech. Kennedy watched the speech on TV. He admired King very much. After the meeting, Kennedy asked King and the other leaders to come to the White House to meet him.

JFK meets Martin Luther King Junior and other march leaders

10   Race to the moon

The US and USSR were on opposite sides in the Cold War. They were against each other in another way too. Each country wanted to be the first to send a man to the moon. This was called the 'Space Race'.

In 1960, President Eisenhower started the Apollo Space Program, and when Kennedy became president, he went on with it. Kennedy thought it was very important for the

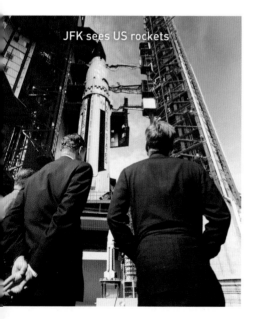

JFK sees US rockets

US to be the leader in the Space Race. He wanted to show the world that the US was a great and strong country.

It cost billions of dollars to send a man into space. On 25 May 1961, Kennedy gave a speech to Congress. He said that it was very important for the US to win the Space Race. By the end of the 1960s, he said, he wanted to send a man to the moon and back. He asked Congress for twenty-two billion dollars for the Apollo Space Program, and Congress agreed to give him the money.

On 12 April 1961, the Soviets sent a man called Yuri Gagarin into space for the first time. Kennedy was worried that the US was getting behind the USSR. He thought that perhaps the Americans and Soviets could work together, and he asked Khrushchev about this at the meeting in Vienna in June 1961. But Khrushchev did not want help from the US. He did not want the Americans to learn about the work that the USSR was doing on space travel, so he said no.

On 12 September 1962, Kennedy made a speech at Rice University in Texas. He told the people why the Apollo Space Program was so important for the US. He said, 'We choose to go to the moon . . . and do the other things, not because they are easy, but because they are hard.'

On 21 July 1969, nearly six years after Kennedy's death, the Americans Neil Armstrong and Edwin Eugene 'Buzz' Aldrin became the first men to walk on the moon. So the US won the Space Race, but Kennedy did not live to see it happen.

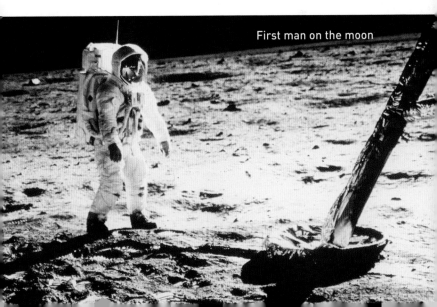

First man on the moon

11   The world in shock

Kennedy started many good things, but he was not able to finish all of them. In November 1963, he and Jackie went to Texas for a political visit. On 22 November, they were driving through the streets of Dallas in an open car. Kennedy and Jackie sat in the back, behind the Governor of Texas, John Connally, and his wife. The driver and another man sat in the front of the car.

The president's car drove very slowly through the streets. Everybody wanted to see the good-looking young president and his beautiful wife. Crowds of smiling people stood on both sides of the streets, waiting for Kennedy and Jackie. At about 12.30 p.m., the president's car entered Elm Street. Suddenly the crowd heard loud shots from a gun. Two bullets hit the president – the first

Dallas, 22 November 1963

in his back and neck, and the other in his head. One bullet hit John Connally.

Kennedy was very badly hurt. The presidential car drove as fast as possible to the Parkland Memorial Hospital. But it was too late. At 1 p.m. Kennedy was dead.

While the car was taking Kennedy to the hospital, the police were busy looking for the killer in the buildings near Elm Street. They entered a building on the corner of Elm Street and Houston Street. In one of the rooms upstairs, they found an open window and a gun lying on the floor. From this room, you could easily look down into the street where the president's car was driving.

The bullets came from this building

Seventy minutes later, the police caught a man called Lee Harvey Oswald. Oswald was twenty-four years old. He said that he did not shoot Kennedy, but the police did not believe him and they took him to the police station. Two days later, the police were getting ready to move Oswald to prison. A large crowd was waiting in the police station to see him. When the police brought Oswald out, a man pushed to the front of the crowd and shot Oswald dead. This man's name was Jack Ruby.

The US government asked the Warren Commission, a group of senators and lawyers, to find out what happened. After some months, they decided that Oswald killed Kennedy, and that he was working alone.

But not everyone believes that. How could a man like Oswald, a nobody, kill the president of the US without help? Many people think that Oswald was working for someone else. But who? The Soviets? Castro? The CIA? There are many different ideas, but nobody will ever know for sure. The only man who knew the true answer – Lee Harvey Oswald – is dead. Jack Ruby is also dead. He became ill in prison and died on 3 January 1967.

Jackie and Caroline say goodbye

12 The years after

Kennedy was president for only about a thousand days. His death was a terrible shock for people around the world. Many saw it happen on TV. A short time before his death, Kennedy was happy and smiling. Then in a few seconds, the US lost a fine young president.

After Kennedy's death, Lyndon B. Johnson became president. He went on with Kennedy's work for equal rights. In 1964, there was an important new law which gave black Americans the same rights as white Americans at work, in schools, restaurants and hotels, and on buses. Many black Americans started going to university, and some got good jobs in law and government. On 20 January 2009, Barack Obama became America's first African-American president.

Others from the Kennedy family became famous too. Kennedy's sister Jean became US Ambassador to Ireland. Kennedy's brother Robert was a US senator, and US Attorney General from 1961 to 1964. His youngest brother, Edward (Ted), was a US senator for forty-seven years.

After Kennedy's death, many people admired Jackie's quiet courage. In 1968, she married Aristotle Onassis, a Greek businessman. After he died in 1975, she returned to America and got a job in New York, where she died in 1994. One of the gardens at the White House is called the Jacqueline Kennedy Garden.

Barack Obama and
Caroline Kennedy

Caroline Kennedy is Kennedy and Jackie's only living child. She is a writer and lawyer, and in 2013 she became US ambassador to Japan. Caroline and her husband, Edwin Arthur Schlossberg, have three children – Rose, John (Jack), and Tatiana. People think that Caroline's older daughter, Rose, looks very like her famous grandmother, Jackie. Kennedy's son, John, was killed in an accident in July 1999 with his wife and his wife's sister. He was flying a small plane which crashed into the sea.

Things did not always go well for Kennedy. Sometimes he had terrible problems because of his back and other illnesses, but he never felt sorry for himself. He made some mistakes, like the Bay of Pigs, but he did his best to learn from them. There were other problems too. He liked women, and women liked him. After he married, he had some relationships with other women. Sometimes this made things very difficult for his government.

But people remember the good things about Kennedy more than the problems. He was a strong, intelligent leader with a lot of courage. He kept the US out of nuclear war, and he tried his best to bring peace to the world. People remember John F. Kennedy not because he was good-looking or charming, or because he was a war hero or won a Pulitzer Prize. They remember him because he was a great president who believed in a better future for the world.

GLOSSARY

admire to think that somebody is very good

Air Force the planes that a country uses for fighting, and the people who fly them

allow to say that somebody can have or do something

ambassador an important person who represents their country in a foreign country

attack to try to hurt or kill somebody

award a prize for somebody who has done something very well

become to begin to be something

believe to think that something is true

bullet a small piece of metal that comes out of a gun

candidate a person who wants to be chosen for something

Catholic a member of the Christian church that follows the Pope in Rome

Central Intelligence Agency (CIA) a part of the US government that collects information about other countries

charming very pleasant or attractive

choose to decide which person or thing you want

citizen a person who belongs to a country or a city

control to have power over something

courage not being afraid when you do something dangerous

Democrat a member of the Democratic Party, one of the two main political parties in the US

divide to make something into smaller parts

election a time when people choose somebody to be a leader

enter to go into something

equal rights the same rights to vote, work, go to school, etc. as everybody else

government a group of people who control a country

hero a person who has done something brave or good

idea a new thought or plan; a picture in your head

illness a problem with the body that makes you ill

intelligent good at learning and thinking

join to become a member of a group or organization

law   a rule of a country that says what people may or may not do;
   (*n*) **lawyer**   someone who helps people with the law
leader   the most important person in a group, a government, etc.
military advisor   a soldier who gives advice about war and fighting
missile   a powerful weapon that is sent through the air;
   missile site   a place where missiles are kept
navy   the ships that a country uses for war and the people who
   work on them
nuclear   using the energy that is made when an atom is broken
part   one of the pieces of something
party   a group of people who have the same ideas about politics
patrol   a group of people that go round a place to see that
   everything is all right
peace   a time when there is no war or fighting
political (*adj*)   connected with government; (*n*) **politician**   a person
   connected with government
problem   something difficult to understand, or find an answer for
promise   to say that you will certainly do something
protect   to keep something safe
relationship   the way people or countries behave with each other
   or how they feel about each other
Republican   a member of the Republican Party, one of the two
   main political parties in the US
Senior   used after the name of a father who has the same name
   as his son
shock   a sudden and unpleasant surprise
space   the area outside the Earth's atmosphere
speech   a talk that you give to a group of people
state   one of the fifty different parts of the US, e.g. California
surrender   to stop fighting because you cannot win
test   to use something to find out if it works well
torpedo   a type of bomb that travels under the water
train (*v*)   to teach somebody to do a job
university   a place where people go to study after they leave school
vote   to choose someone in an election
war   fighting between armies of different countries
weapon   something that you use to fight with

ACTIVITIES

Before Reading

1 **How much do you know about John F. Kennedy's life? Circle one answer in each sentence.**

   1 Kennedy was president of the US for *eight years / nearly three years / less than two years*.
   2 Kennedy's family first came to the US from *Spain / France / Ireland*.
   3 Kennedy's father was a *farmer / businessman / doctor*.
   4 Kennedy's wife was called *Susan / Jackie / Janet*.
   5 Kennedy died in *1963 / 1974 / 1985*.
   6 The president after Kennedy was *George Bush / Barack Obama / Lyndon B. Johnson*.

2 **How many of these people have you heard of? Match the people to the descriptions.**

   Fidel Castro, Caroline Kennedy, Robert Kennedy, Nikita Khrushchev, Martin Luther King Junior

   1 He was leader of Cuba when Kennedy was president.
   2 He wanted equal rights for black Americans.
   3 He helped his brother win the presidential election.
   4 He was leader of the USSR during the Cold War.
   5 She is Kennedy's only living child.

ACTIVITIES

While Reading

Read Chapters 1 and 2. Are these sentences true (T) or false (F)? Rewrite the false ones with the correct information.

1 John F. Kennedy was forty-two when he became president of the US.
2 Mount Kennedy is in Canada.
3 Two million Irish people died because they had nothing to eat.
4 Joe and Rose Kennedy called their first son Jack.
5 The Kennedy family had two homes.
6 Jack was not popular at the Choate School.
7 The leader of Italy in the 1930s was Adolf Hitler.

Read Chapter 3, then put these sentences in the right order.

1 A Japanese warship hit the *PT-109*.
2 Some islanders found the men.
3 The US government gave Jack an award.
4 Jack joined the US Navy.
5 Jack pulled McMahon to an island.
6 Joe Kennedy was killed.
7 Jack became leader of the *PT-109*.
8 The men jumped into the sea.

Read Chapters 4 and 5, then match these halves of sentences.

1 Congress is one of the three parts of . . .
2 Richard Nixon was presidential candidate for . . .
3 The presidential elections happened . . .
4 Kennedy met Jackie at a dinner party . . .
5 Jackie had a job . . .
6 The White House is the home of . . .
7 Caroline and ten other children went to school . . .

a in New York.
b in the White House.
c the US government.
d with a newspaper.
e the US president.
f in November 1960.
g the Republican party.

Read Chapter 6. Choose the best question-word for these questions, and then answer them.

How many / What / When / Where / Who

1 _____ was Nikita Khrushchev?
2 _____ did Kennedy and Khrushchev meet in June 1961?
3 _____ people left East Berlin between 1947 and 1961?
4 _____ did the East German soldiers build in August 1961?
5 _____ did Kennedy visit West Berlin?

Read Chapter 7. Complete the sentences with the names of these people or places.

Bay of Pigs, Cuba, Eisenhower, Europe, Kennedy, Khrushchev, Turkey

1 The US president before Kennedy was _____.
2 Ships carrying about 1,500 Cuban soldiers arrived at the _____.
3 Fidel Castro, leader of the government in _____, was a Communist.
4 _____ sent two letters to Kennedy.
5 After the Bay of Pigs, _____ did not agree to everything his military advisors told him.
6 The US had some nuclear missile sites in _____.
7 People in London and countries in _____ held meetings against the US.

Read Chapters 8 and 9, then circle the correct words.

1 Young people in the Peace Corps help people in *the US / other countries.*
2 Ngô Đình Diệm was president of *South / North* Vietnam.
3 The army officers said that they would *shoot / protect* Diệm.
4 When Kennedy became president, black Americans *had / did not have* the same rights as white Americans.
5 Robert Kennedy sent *hundreds / thousands* of soldiers to protect James Meredith.

Read Chapters 10 and 11. Then circle *a*, *b* or *c*.

1 The US and USSR wanted to be first to reach _____.
   a) the sun   b) the moon   c) Mars

2 The first man to go into space was _____.
   a) Buzz Aldrin   b) Neil Armstrong   c) Yuri Gagarin

3 The city of Dallas is _____.
   a) in Texas   b) near Washington   c) in Florida

4 The president's car was traveling _____.
   a) quickly   b) slowly   c) very fast

5 The number of bullets that hit Kennedy was _____.
   a) one   b) two   c) three

6 The Warren Commission said Oswald was working _____.
   a) for the FBI   b) for Castro   c) alone

7 Jack Ruby died _____.
   a) in a police station   b) in prison   c) in the street

Read Chapter 12, then answer the questions.

1 When did Barack Obama become president?

2 Who else in the Kennedy family became famous?

3 Who was Jackie's second husband?

4 What did Jackie do after Onassis died?

5 Who is Caroline Kennedy married to?

6 What happened to Kennedy's son?

7 What do people remember most about Kennedy?

ACTIVITIES

After Reading

1 Find these words in the wordsearch below, and draw lines through them. The words go from left to right, and from top to bottom.

ambassador, attack, candidate, courage, Democrat, election, hero, lawyer, peace, politician, promise, speech, torpedo, vote, war

C	P	O	L	I	T	I	C	I	A	N
O	E	A	A	S	O	K	A	N	T	A
U	A	O	W	T	R	W	N	H	T	M
R	C	A	Y	T	P	Y	D	O	A	B
A	E	P	E	U	E	R	I	C	C	A
G	O	R	R	U	D	N	D	T	K	S
E	V	O	T	E	O	W	A	R	R	S
D	E	M	O	C	R	A	T	Y	C	A
A	N	I	D	O	F	H	E	R	O	D
O	R	S	Y	S	P	E	E	C	H	O
E	L	E	C	T	I	O	N	O	U	R

1 Which three words are types of jobs?
2 Which two nouns are the opposite of each other?

Write down all the letters that do not have lines through them. Begin with the first line, and go across each line to the end. There are 32 letters, making a phrase of 9 words.

3 Who said these words?
4 When did he say them?

2 Read these two newspaper reports about things which happened in Kennedy's life. Complete them using the words below (one word for each gap).

admire, because, choose, country, crowd, excited, great, hard, leaders, moon, peace, rights, Space, speech, spoke, streets, University, walk, White, win

---

13 SEPTEMBER 1962

THE RACE IS ON! SAYS PRESIDENT

Yesterday, President John F. Kennedy _____ to an _____ crowd at Rice _____ in Texas. He said that America would _____ the Space Race, and put a man on the _____ before the USSR. 'The Apollo _____ Program is very important for our _____,' he said. 'We _____ to go to the moon . . . and do the other things, not _____ they are easy, but because they are _____.'

---

29 August 1963

President meets King

Yesterday was a _____ day for black Americans. A _____ of about 250,000 people walked in _____ through the _____ of Washington. One of the leaders of the _____, Martin Luther King, gave a _____ about equal _____ for all Americans. Later, President Kennedy asked King and other _____ to come to the _____ House. 'I greatly _____ your work,' the President told King.

3 **Do you agree or disagree with these sentences? Why?**

1 The Kennedys are a very unlucky family.
2 Lee Harvey Oswald was working alone.
3 Kennedy was the greatest US president of all time.
4 Kennedy's biggest mistake was the Bay of Pigs.
5 The best thing that Kennedy did was to start the Peace Corps.

4 **You are going to make a film about Kennedy's life. Answer these questions about your film.**

1 Who are the main characters?
2 Which actors would you choose to play these characters?
3 Which parts of Kennedy's life would be the most important parts in your film?

5 **Find out some more information about one of these people. Give a talk to your class about their life.**

• Martin Luther King Junior
• Fidel Castro
• Jackie Kennedy (Onassis)
• Nikita Khrushchev
• Robert Kennedy

Here are some websites that can help you:
http://www.thekingcenter.org
http://en.wikipedia.org/wiki/Fidel_Castro
http://en.wikipedia.org/wiki/Nikita_Khrushchev
http://www.jfklibrary.org/JFK/Life-of-Jacqueline-B-Kennedy.aspx
http://www.spartacus.schoolnet.co.uk/USAkennedyR.htm

ABOUT THE AUTHOR

Anne Collins is an experienced teacher and ELT author. She has written coursebooks and over forty Graded Readers, from adaptations of classics, contemporary novels, movies, and plays to original stories and biographies.

Anne's teaching career began in Greece, where she worked in a school on the island of Kos. She lived with a Greek family for a year, which gave her the perfect opportunity to learn some Modern Greek. After two years working as a courier for a Greek tourist company, she decided to return to teaching. Since then, she has lived and worked in Saudi Arabia, Turkey, China, and Oman, and she has also taught in other countries such as Russia, Spain, and Austria.

Anne also works as a freelance journalist and very much enjoys interviewing people. She believes that everyone has an interesting story to tell. She has written about a wide range of people in Oman with unusual lives, ranging from action heroes and sportsmen and women to writers, inventors, and directors of charities. Her interviews have been published in magazines and by online news organizations. In 2011 she was awarded the 'Member of the Year' award by an Omani online news organization, *Knowledge Oman*.

One of Anne's many interests is American history, particularly the lives of American Presidents. One of her favorite Presidents is John F. Kennedy, because for JFK the most important thing was world peace. She completely agrees with his reasoning for establishing the world-famous Peace Corps – that the best way of promoting international understanding is for individuals to experience the culture of another country by living and working there.

Anne's other interests include traveling, travel writing, music, film, concerts, opera, and piano playing.

OXFORD BOOKWORMS LIBRARY

Classics • Crime & Mystery • Factfiles • Fantasy & Horror
Human Interest • Playscripts • Thriller & Adventure
True Stories • World Stories

The OXFORD BOOKWORMS LIBRARY provides enjoyable reading in English, with a wide range of classic and modern fiction, non-fiction, and plays. It includes original and adapted texts in seven carefully graded language stages, which take learners from beginner to advanced level. An overview is given on the next pages.

All Stage 1 titles are available as audio recordings, as well as over eighty other titles from Starter to Stage 6. All Starters and many titles at Stages 1 to 4 are specially recommended for younger learners. Every Bookworm is illustrated, and Starters and Factfiles have full-colour illustrations.

The OXFORD BOOKWORMS LIBRARY also offers extensive support. Each book contains an introduction to the story, notes about the author, a glossary, and activities. Additional resources include tests and worksheets, and answers for these and for the activities in the books. There is advice on running a class library, using audio recordings, and the many ways of using Oxford Bookworms in reading programmes. Resource materials are available on the website <www.oup.com/elt/gradedreaders>.

The *Oxford Bookworms Collection* is a series for advanced learners. It consists of volumes of short stories by well-known authors, both classic and modern. Texts are not abridged or adapted in any way, but carefully selected to be accessible to the advanced student.

You can find details and a full list of titles in the *Oxford Bookworms Library Catalogue* and *Oxford English Language Teaching Catalogues*, and on the website <www.oup.com/elt/gradedreaders>.

THE OXFORD BOOKWORMS LIBRARY
GRADING AND SAMPLE EXTRACTS

STARTER • 250 HEADWORDS

present simple – present continuous – imperative –
can/cannot, must – *going to* (future) – simple gerunds …

Her phone is ringing – but where is it?

Sally gets out of bed and looks in her bag. No phone. She looks under the bed. No phone. Then she looks behind the door. There is her phone. Sally picks up her phone and answers it. *Sally's Phone*

STAGE 1 • 400 HEADWORDS

… past simple – coordination with *and*, *but*, *or* –
subordination with *before, after, when, because, so* …

I knew him in Persia. He was a famous builder and I worked with him there. For a time I was his friend, but not for long. When he came to Paris, I came after him – I wanted to watch him. He was a very clever, very dangerous man. *The Phantom of the Opera*

STAGE 2 • 700 HEADWORDS

… present perfect – *will* (future) – *(don't) have to, must not, could* –
comparison of adjectives – simple *if* clauses – past continuous –
tag questions – *ask/tell* + infinitive …

While I was writing these words in my diary, I decided what to do. I must try to escape. I shall try to get down the wall outside. The window is high above the ground, but I have to try. I shall take some of the gold with me – if I escape, perhaps it will be helpful later. *Dracula*

STAGE 3 • 1000 HEADWORDS

… should, may – present perfect continuous – *used to* – past perfect –
causative – relative clauses – indirect statements …

Of course, it was most important that no one should see
Colin, Mary, or Dickon entering the secret garden. So Colin
gave orders to the gardeners that they must all keep away
from that part of the garden in future. *The Secret Garden*

STAGE 4 • 1400 HEADWORDS

… past perfect continuous – passive (simple forms) –
would conditional clauses – indirect questions –
relatives with *where/when* – gerunds after prepositions/phrases …

I was glad. Now Hyde could not show his face to the world
again. If he did, every honest man in London would be proud
to report him to the police. *Dr Jekyll and Mr Hyde*

STAGE 5 • 1800 HEADWORDS

… future continuous – future perfect –
passive (modals, continuous forms) –
would have conditional clauses – modals + perfect infinitive …

If he had spoken Estella's name, I would have hit him. I was so
angry with him, and so depressed about my future, that I could
not eat the breakfast. Instead I went straight to the old house.
Great Expectations

STAGE 6 • 2500 HEADWORDS

… passive (infinitives, gerunds) – advanced modal meanings –
clauses of concession, condition

When I stepped up to the piano, I was confident. It was as if I
knew that the prodigy side of me really did exist. And when I
started to play, I was so caught up in how lovely I looked that
I didn't worry how I would sound. *The Joy Luck Club*

BOOKWORMS
FACTFILES
STAGE 2

Leonardo da Vinci

ALEX RAYNHAM

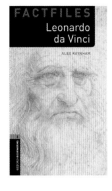

'What does the world look like from the moon?' 'How do our bodies work?' 'Is it possible for people to fly?' 'Can I make a horse of bronze that is 8 metres tall?' 'How can we have cleaner cities?' All his life, Leonardo da Vinci asked questions. We know him as a great artist, but he was also one of the great thinkers of all time, and even today, doctors and scientists are still learning from his ideas. Meet the man who made a robot lion, wrote backwards, and tried to win a war by moving a river . . .

BOOKWORMS
FACTFILES
STAGE 3

The USA

ALISON BAXTER

Everybody knows about the United States of America. You can see its films, hear its music, and eat its food just about everywhere. Cowboys, jazz, hamburgers, the Stars and Stripes – that's the United States.

But it's a country with many stories to tell. Stories of busy cities, beautiful forests and parks. Stories of a country that fought against Britain, and then against itself, to make the United States of today. Stories of rich and poor, black and white, Native American and immigrant. And the story of what it is like to be an American today . . .